Right Pieces, Wrong Puzzle

Puzzle

The Synergy of Passion & Purpose

Eric A. Rollerson

Eric A. Rollerson

DEDICATION

Dear Grandma or "Mama", as I typically called you, I gladly dedicate this book to you. This special honor is specifically reserved for you because you were the catalyst that ignited my fiery affinity for books. Grandma, I am an avid reader to this day because you taught me how to read at the age of three. You always challenged me to learn and I am better for it. Whenever I didn't know the meaning of a word, you consistently made me look it up in the dictionary and use it in a sentence of my own. Beyond that, Grandma, you remained the very foundation of my faith until I was able to discover its meaning for myself. As I grew up, I knew that if anyone could get a prayer through to God, it was you, Grandma. For all your benevolent prayers, your peerless love, your impeccable support, your constant nosiness, and even your "out-of-love" scoldings, with every ounce of my being, I say thank you.

Thank you, because you played a significant role in molding me into the man I am today—especially regarding my need to always have a bottle of hand-sanitizer and a can of Lysol nearby -- ha. You were the Doctor of Disinfecting everything! There simply are no words in existence that can adequately convey how much I miss you and your handwritten letters. There are no words to even begin explaining how much I love you. In the end, even words such as "illustrious" or "venerable" pale in comparison to any effort in trying to describe you. Frankie Mae Rollerson, you truly were one of a kind. Besides riding in the car or sitting in the living room with Papa (Paw-Paw) and I, Heaven is the only place more fitting for you and a woman of your caliber. "Mama", I dedicate my first published title to you.

Love Eric

CONTENTS

ACKNOWLEDGMENTS

If I could thank everyone who has been significant in my life thus far, I'd end up writing a whole other book. However, I will extend my best effort to acknowledge the most appropriate parties below.

I must give all the glory and honor to my savior Jesus Christ who is the very radix of my resilience. Without him, not only would this book not have been possible, but *I* would not be possible.

To my Papa (Paw-Paw), Lonell Rollerson, for literally everything you've done for me. I probably wouldn't know my right from my left if it weren't for you. Paw-Paw, you have always been there for me no matter what, and you are a quintessential example of a man of integrity. I love you with every fiber in my being. Thank you.

To my amazing parents, Eric and Erma Rollerson, for being my biggest supporters and for always encouraging me. You two are the sources of my motivation and work-ethic. Your consistent love and constant prayers have sustained me through the worst of times. How did I, as a son, get so blessed? I love you two more than you'll ever know. Thank you.

To my siblings: Scott, Tashayla, and Aaron, for being both my headaches and my cheerleaders. Our relationship and shared memories are beyond terrestrial comprehension. With every accomplishment of mine, y'all are always there to boost me and it fills my cup to the brim. I love y'all a ton. Thank you.

To my beloved nephew, Ll'Xander, for making me the proudest uncle on earth. You are one of the primary reasons why I work so hard. By the time you get my age, I want this world to practically be at your feet. You are so intelligent, radiant, talented, and kind, there's no wonder I claim you as my "son". Uncle loves you to the moon back. Thank you.

To "The Community", for all the memories, the laughs, the tears, and most importantly for being my family away from home. You all push me to be the best that I can be. The love I have for each one of you is indescribable. Thank you.

To my non-OU/commuting best friends, for never allowing distance to change the dynamic of our friendship. Your support means everything to me—especially when you take the time to drive to Norman to be with me. I love you all so much. Thank you.

To my former teachers, counselors, and principles, you know who you are, for always believing in me. The cards, notes, texts, and inspirational chats have been crucial in helping me get through times of doubt. You have undeniably been instrumental in my success. Thank you.

To Tyler Roberts, my former resident, who unwittingly inspired the title of this book. Thank you.

Last but most certainly not the least, to my adviser, my mentor; my campus mother, my friend; and the Queen herself, Mrs. Crystal Perkins Carter. There are no words to perfectly articulate my gratitude for you. Without you, I couldn't have brought my book to life. I will treasure your gems of wisdom and guidance forever. Thank you.

INTRODUCTION

It's been said time and time again: you need to know what you want to do before you get to college. They say that the main reason you need to go to college is so that you can get a degree that will allow you to make a lot of money. I must admit, I too, believed these statements to be true once upon a time.

I thought that by my senior year in high school, I had to be one-hundred percent sure of the profession I wanted to seek once I entered the collegiate world. With tunnel vision, I had my mind set on making my coins. Just to be clear, in addition to 'making my coins', I may use slang terms like: making bread, making bank, and securing the bag. For those of you who are unfamiliar, these are simply colloquialisms constructed by millennials that refer to the process of generating income and solidifying financial stability.

I will also add, for future reference, if there are any phrases that seem unconventional or out of place, I assure you, they belong there. More often than not, they are just other modern-day colloquialisms naturally added to my personal vernacular and used by those belonging to younger generations.

Getting back on track, in hindsight, I wish I had known those statements were false, and ultimately misleading. I could have saved myself from some sleepless nights and the tons of pressure that threatened to suffocate me. But what would be the fun be in that? Life just wouldn't be its perfect, sunshiny-self without a few storm clouds filled with ice-cold rain to throw a wrench in your plans and knock you off course.

Now, I'm sure I've bored you long enough. You're probably anxious to read about the part that tells you college is going to be a piece of cake if you do this "one thing". Or, the part where I give you the golden ticket that allows you skip to the end, and the journey is over before it even begins. Unfortunately, neither of those two wishful thinking ideas exist—at least not in this book. If you happen to run across one that does, let me know. I wouldn't mind taking a little peeky-peek myself -- lol. Although I may not have the shortcuts to this thing, I can give you some gems of advice that will hopefully help you to not only learn how to play this game of life and college, but also ultimately set you up to win.

Eric A. Rollerson

CHAPTER 1

Puzzle Piece: Find Your Passion Pt. 1

If you had to choose a career that you did for the rest of your life but did not get paid for it, what would it be? *You're probably wondering what this has to do with finding your passion, right? Well, this is a great way to do it.* I typically pose this question to anyone who is struggling to pick a major or who can't decide on what they want to do with their lives post-college. This is a question that I have even asked -- and answered -- myself. The reason I like to ask this question is because it forces an individual to remove money from the equation and truly zero-in on the thing(s) they would do for a living in the absence of it. This method works well for some. For others, not so much. Whether or not you are able to zero-in on a particular career or field of expertise, by looking beyond the money, you will discover that there is much more to life than "getting paper".

Before we continue down this path of career conceptualization, I must apologize. But before I do that, I need to make something clear. Yes, I meant *we* when I wrote "we continue down this path." I said *we* because I want you to know that you are not alone on this journey. I want you to know that I am right there with you. Physically, I may be absent; however, as you read the words on this page, trust me when I say we're in this thing together. I am on this journey to explore my passions and fulfill my purpose, just as some of you who are reading this right now might be. Remember this: **the journey does not merely end when we find our passion and purpose. We simply begin a new one as we extend our hands to help someone else find their own**.

Now, where was I? Ah yes, I believe I owe you -- my readers -- an apology. I apologize because I haven't been as forthcoming with you as I should have been. You haven't heard my story. I never told you how I came to grasp the concept of "**finding your passion.**" What is my passion? How did I find it? Am I still searching? Please, stay tuned because all shall be revealed in time.

CHAPTER 2

Puzzle Piece: Find Your Passion Pt. 2

Before I first stepped foot onto the University of Oklahoma's campus, let me tell you, Eric had it all figured out. I knew that I was going to major in Psychology, go to medical school, and become a Pediatric Psychiatrist. In words that can accurately articulate my thoughts back then, I was going to be "making that bread." And you couldn't tell me nothing! You want to know why? It's a long story, and you're probably going to laugh at me, but I think I have a couple of minutes to spare to share this story.

This story unfolds while I was still in high school. Keep in mind, I hadn't yet matured into the man I am today. Although I thought I had everything figured out, high school Eric had no idea what was in store for him. Going back in time, I can vividly picture a moment during senior year. I had just gotten my class schedule. Everything was perfect except for one class. The one class I was looking forward to was indeed on my schedule, but the teacher I was hoping to have was not. At that moment, it felt as if multiple red alarms were loudly sounding off in my head; the blinding fluorescent lights were flashing back and forth like somebody was trying to take ten thousand photos of me with the flash on. For two years in a row, I'd been taught by Ms. Hollingsworth. *It's Mrs. Sullivan now, but I will always know her as Ms. H.* Much to my chagrin, instead of seeing Ms. H.'s name, I saw Ms. Peterson's. I remember being absolutely mortified for about the first twelve seconds -- lol, then I ran straight to the counselor's office to get a class-switch form. There was no way I was about to stay in Ms. Peterson's class when I should be in class with Ms. H. After that, I just had to wait patiently to get moved to the appropriate teacher's class.

§

So funnily enough, the day before all the class-switch forms were due, I ran back to my counselor to have mine canceled. Now why on earth would I do that? Well, I'll tell you. While I sat in Ms. Peterson's class, just biding my time until I was switched over to Ms. H's, I met a girl named Sara. We initially started talking because she was friends with my younger brother. After having a couple of conversations with her, she told me that her dad is a psychiatrist. *Starting to see where this is going? No? Let's carry on then.* So, Sara tells me that her dad is a psychiatrist, and that he has this major research facility connected to the psychiatric practice. She tells me that he could hook me up with an internship when I started attending OU. From that moment, I had convinced myself that this was a sign from above, and that I needed to stay in that class to stay close to this girl. I know it may seem outlandish and totally bananas, but that's what ultimately led to my staying in Ms. Peterson's class. Don't get me wrong, notwithstanding the potential beneficial networking connections she possessed, I eventually built my own friendship with Sara. On top of that, I could not have made it through that class had it not been for Sara, my girl Haylee Smoot who kept me sane and entertained, and the cool little freshmen: Garrett, Maddison, and Cameron. At the end of the day, once I gave her a chance, Ms. Peterson wasn't half bad.

With that story out of the way, let me tell you this. Being in high school does not mean you aren't mature enough to make important life decisions such as figuring out your future profession. Nor does it equate to your ability to fully comprehend those same important life decisions. I understand that the high school version of myself didn't really have it together like he thought, but that was me. I personally wasn't ready for such a demand -- you might be. Even if you're not, that's okay too.

Overall, understand that this story, and those to come, are as unique to me as yours will be to you. The mistaken path I eventually set sail upon was just a tangible idea that made me feel special, prepared, and well put together. It always felt so good to tell my family, friends, teachers, and strangers at the store that I was going to the prestigious University of Oklahoma to become a doctor. In saying all of that, at the end of the day, all I wanted to do was help children. I thought that if I could help people struggling with different issues while they were young, they would have a better shot at what we all perceive to be a normal adult life. In the prolific words of Frederick Douglass, "It's easier to build strong children than to repair broken men." Although my path has since changed, my passion for helping the youth remains.

Unbeknownst to me, I had pinpointed a passion of mine that I wanted to implement in my future professional life after OU. The thing is, I just didn't recognize it as "my passion" if that makes sense. Thinking back, as I approached my freshman year at OU, I wish someone would have warned me that I was in for a dramatic wake up call. Unexpectedly, this new journey would lead me down the path of self-discovery. I didn't know it then, but I already possessed the right pieces I needed in order to feel complete and happy in life. Problem is, I was too busy trying to jam them into the wrong puzzle.

For clarity, I use the analogy of a puzzle to simply illustrate that our lives are like puzzles. In order to feel whole, and complete our puzzle, we must fill in the missing spaces with the pieces that are right for us. The wrong pieces won't work. Think of it like this: you can't complete a puzzle that's missing a square, by inserting a triangle or a rectangle.

CHAPTER 3

Puzzle Piece: Find Your Passion Pt. 3

Would you believe me if I told you that I discovered my life's path just by taking one class? If you don't, that's too bad because that's exactly what happened. Julius Caesar once said, "Experience is the teacher of all things." I have to say that I agree with our old friend Caesar. This class sent me on a wild goose chase, and I ended up in the Chattahoochee River. In other words, your boy was lost and confused. What class would dare try to impede my future success? Well, that would be Pre-Calculus Trigonometry. Anyone who knows me understands that I really do not mesh well with the subject. I will always openly admit to my disdain for math. Now, I talk a good game when it comes to my opinion about math; however, the reality is that when it's taught well, I'm actually pretty good at it -- if I do say so myself. *And I do say so.* At first, I didn't think much of it because I had taken this very class in high school and aced it. However, I quickly realized that I had prematurely disregarded the potential difficulty level of this university Pre-Calculus Trigonometry class.

Like I said before, I just knew that I was going to do well in this math course because I had taken it prior to college. Because of my ridiculous amount of overconfidence, I neglected to study for the first exam. Instead of seeking help from my professor, the campus' math center, or tutors, I winged it. Luckily for me, I ended up scoring a 76%. And let me tell you, I was so relieved. Instead of being upset that I didn't earn my usual A, I was remarkably calm. The feeling was so unfamiliar to me concerning such a low grade in my mind, it actually made me shudder. But, as fast as one might blink their eye, the feeling was gone. I took my "L" and kept it pushing. It wouldn't be until after the second test that I became fully cognizant of the fact that the "L" I took on the first test was nothing. To describe it, it'd be like comparing tiny ripples on the surface of a pond, to massive waves in the ocean being tossed back and forth by the winds of a raging tempest.

§

After the first exam, I immediately began to prepare for the ensuing battle against the second exam. I armed myself to the hilt with the weapons specially designed for this type of fight. This was war. I was not going to allow myself to be caught unaware, unprepared, and unable to perform to the best of my abilities -- not again. This time around, things were going to be different; I was going to pass this next test with flying colors. With that being said, over the coming weeks, I frequently visited my professor's office hours, I went to our math center; I got involved with a study group; I even got some extra tutoring on the side. As that fateful and dreaded day finally arrived, I courageously marched to the battlegrounds. Even as a thunderstorm rolled in and unleashed its fury in the form of freezing rain, I continued to march. Even though this untimely torrential downpour completely drenched me and everything I wore, I continued to march. As I finally arrived at the frontline, I made my way to my seat. Shoes squeaking and all, I sat down and then the war began. As the clock struck nine o'clock, the exam time had expired. The battle was officially over. I stood up, turned my test in at the front of the immense testing room, and made my way to the exit. Completely soaked to the bone and utterly mind-wiped, I walked my muddy feet to the exit. I pushed open the doors of freedom and inhaled the fragrance of sweet victory permeating throughout the brisk night air.

As soon as I was able to shrug off my wet clothes and shower, I hopped smooth in the bed and fell right asleep. I think that was some of the best sleep I had gotten since coming to OU. I was able to sleep so comfortably because I knew I had aced my Pre-calculus Trigonometry exam. I believed that I had earned the right to enjoy this victory of mine with some well-deserved rest.

§

Two weeks passed and the results from the exam were handed back to us in class. I was so excited and anxious to see the A I made that I didn't even turn over my paper for like five minutes. Y'all can't tell me that wasn't silly of me -- hah! Like why didn't I just turn the paper over, see my good grade, and go on about my day? For whatever reason, maybe to stall some more, I started conversing with my friend Arely Ramirez. Unfortunately for her, she didn't do as well on her test as I knew I had done. I felt so bad for her because I knew how hard she had studied. I decided to console her with the cliché, "It's going to be okay. You'll do better next time" speech. Shortly after that, not being able to contain the anticipation effervescing on the inside of me any longer, I turned my paper over to reveal my A -- only it wasn't an A. It wasn't even a B -- or a C. The bubbly feeling I just had a moment before had fizzled out instantaneously. With my eyes bursting from their sockets and my mouth hanging to the ground -- *and I mean all the way on the ground* -- I sat there in silence. Petrified. Stupefied.

Disconcerted. Flabbergasted. These are only a sample of the words I can call upon from my vocabulary reservoir to attempt to describe the emotions that were chaotically swarming around in my brain. Honestly, there was nothing that could begin to help me comprehend and cope with the grim reality of that big, oversized F that I saw at the top of my paper.

I was truly at a loss for words. The only thought running rampant through my mind was, *"How in the world did I fail this exam?"* I know they say that seeing is believing, but I can promise you that I surely didn't want to believe what I saw. As I grudgingly made it back to my room, I could feel the cold, dark tentacles of depression and disappointment desperately reaching out to strangle me. I just couldn't believe that all my preparation had been for naught. I remember leaving my room to go sit in the study lounge; I didn't want my roommate to see the warm, salty tears that started to slide down the side of my face. Y'all, to be honest, I was ready to throw in the towel. I was ready to go off to some faraway place because I couldn't accept being a failure. All these thoughts kept racing through my head. *"How did I graduate high school with a 4.0 GPA? How was I a member of the National Honors Society? How did I score advanced on all my state tests but get to college and flunk out? Were all of my previous accomplishments nothing but a lie?"*

These were the same self-destructive questions I repeatedly asked myself with no clue as to how I should, or even could, answer them. I couldn't answer them because *I* was the one everybody always expected to do so well in college. *I* was the one everybody knew was going to be successful in life. "Eric is going to do this." "Eric is going to be that." If I had a dollar for every single time I heard that, boy! I would be King Midas rich by now. *But like I was saying* -- I couldn't answer those questions because I knew that there were too many people believing in me. I couldn't entertain and succumb to such volatile thoughts.

So, I called the only person who could bring me back to center and get me straight. I called my grandma. I could literally write a whole book just about her because she's been that instrumental in helping me get this far in my life. As I spoke to my grandma, I gave her the run-down on the whole math situation. I spilled my guts to her about the dark, sinister thoughts prowling around in my head, the amount of stress I was under, how TIRED I was, and how I didn't know what I was going to do since I was failing Pre-calculus Trigonometry. I needed to pass the class in order to graduate! I told her all of that. And you know what? She told me what I knew she was going to say the moment I called her. She didn't give me a lecture; she didn't get upset; she didn't even say she was disappointed. Instead, as calm as the eye of a hurricane, she said seven little words: "It's going to be okay. Trust God." When I say my tears dried up like wet paint on a hot summer day, and my nose quit running like a car out of gas, I fixed my face real quick. Like what could I possibly say after that? Nothing. And that's exactly what I said -- nothing. As simple as they were, those seven words were incredibly profound. I didn't know how I was going to do it, but I was going to get my life and get it with a quickness. I started to remember that I didn't come to OU to just to go back home after the first semester. No ma'am, no ham, no turkey. I was determined to figure out which pieces I needed to complete this college/life puzzle that currently had me confounded.

CHAPTER 4

Puzzle Piece: Find Your Passion Pt. 4

Are y'all still with me? I know that I've told y'all a couple of stories already, but if you bear with me for a few more, I promise it'll all make sense in the end. I'm sharing them with you so that you'll understand that the road to obtaining the *right* pieces to your own puzzle isn't always going to be sunshine and rainbows. There are going to be some mountains to climb, and they're going to be high. Sometimes, you're going to find yourself in a valley so deep, you didn't know things could get so low. On top of that, you may find yourself having to swim across a vast ocean of unforeseen events. When you get to the moments when you must swim, I suggest you grab a life-vest, grab some wayward piece of floating wood, or, *in my Erykah Badu voice* you better call Tyrone -- I don't know, do something. Just don't call me because I can't help you swim -- lol. If you fool with me, we're both going to be under the water, okurrrr! I'm totally kidding -- lol. If you ever need me, I'll most definitely do the best that I can to help you navigate through any situations that come your way. Even if it's a fifty-foot tidal wave towering over both us, at least we'll be gone together, right? I said all of that to make a point: each of my personal stories has been paramount in helping me gather the *right* pieces to my puzzle. So please y'all, don't fall asleep on me just yet.

§

So back to the story. After miserably failing my test, I thought I had lost the war. However, I soon came to realize that I had only lost one mere battle. The war could yet be won, and this soldier needed to jump back onto the battlefield and continue fighting. Wounded as I was, I did just that.

§

The following week, I went to speak with one of my tutors about possibly changing my major. I was curious to know if I could change major but stay pre-med, thereby continuing on my path to be a psychiatrist. You would think that after that exam's results and seeing all the work I had put toward it end up being in vain, I would have realized that something was wrong with the degree track I was on. I will, however, give my poor little freshman self some credit; I did recognize that I needed to change my major. Fortunately, my freshman self was able to pick up on that aspect of things. So, as I was talking to my tutor about the different possibilities, he gave me some advice: I should switch my major to Biology. At the time, I didn't want to hear this. Furthermore, he told me I would have to take almost 15 extra hours of science courses on top of my Psychology degree requirements if I stayed with this major. When he told me that, I almost flipped the script! I was so mad at the fact that the degree I wanted to pursue required me to do more hours than the ones specified on the degree sheet. He also told me that if I switched to Biology, I could make some kind of deal with the Air Force that would result in them paying for medical school. This would mean that I would have to work for them as a doctor for four years.

Y'all, understand this. If you tell a broke, confused freshman like me something like that, know that they are going to lose it! They'll be jumping out of their seats and running the next person over like a 250 lbs. linemen to sign up for such a "great" deal. I said "great" because my tutor never really explained to me how this supposed deal really worked. Now I know that it wasn't the right deal for me. If one of y'all decide to try this deal, and it really does pan out, email me, call me, or come find me, say something -- lol. However you get in contact with me, just let me know so we can hang out, Dr. Whatever-your-last-name is.

Anyway, following through with changing my major to Biology and signing my soul away to the Air Force for four years was a huge decision. This was a decision I didn't want to make without consulting someone in my life who wanted the best for me, and that I trusted to keep it 100% with me. This time, I called my papa (pronounced paw-paw). I could write a book about him, too, because he's also that important to me. Now, concerning this deal proposed by the tutor, my grandpa wasn't even trying to hear it, y'all. In more ways than one, he basically said something along the lines of, "Nah, I don't know about all of that. There has to be something else you can do. I wouldn't trust it. I know you think you know what's best because you're in college now, but trust me on this." All I could say was, "OK." Although I wasn't completely sure about what I was going to do, I felt so much better after talking this dilemma over with my papa.

§

As the days rolled on, I found myself becoming more restless. Here I was, in the middle of October, still sitting in a math class that I knew I had to get out of. With no idea as to what I was going to change my major to, the mounting stress was beginning to constrict me like a deadly reticulated python. I had to break free of this unceremonious grip. Otherwise, I knew that I would become overwhelmed and undoubtedly be consumed. But how? How on earth was I going to escape this seemingly endless cycle of burdensome and unnecessary stress?

Well, fortunately for me, I had met a friend by the name of Caroline Bennett who just so happened to be the reigning Miss Black OU at the time. When I tell you this woman was deeply connected all across campus, this woman was connected! She was friends with deans, vice presidents, department chairs, etc. To say the least, Caroline practically knew everybody. I always thought it was fascinating to know someone who knew so many important people. It never occurred to me that my friendship with Caroline would eventually lead me to the office a woman that would not only help me find my **passion**, but my **purpose**.

One day, as I was walking back to Couch Center (an OU residence hall) from my late Spanish class, I saw Caroline sitting by the café. We instantly struck up a conversation. Toward the end of this conversation, I told her about my math class and asked her if she knew anyone who could help me. Unsurprisingly, she happened to know just the person. This woman was none other than Mrs. Crystal Perkins Carter.

The first time I met Mrs. Carter, I didn't know who she was. As I walked into a student orientation session for BSA (Black Student Association), I noticed a woman in the back of the room. She was so far tucked into shadows I couldn't clearly see her face. It was almost as if she was trying to avoid being seen. Mind you, I had never seen her in my life -- yet my spirit told me she was important. As I gazed in her direction, I could feel something inside of me begin to buzz. It felt like electricity coursing through my veins. At one point, I felt as if I was going to turn into Storm from the X-men and start hurling lightning bolts across the room.

Even as multiple presenters got up to speak, my attention kept reverting to the same woman in the back of the room. Internally, I began to speak to my spirit. *Who is this woman? What are you trying to tell me? Why is all my focus being drawn to her?* Not too long after I finished conversing within myself, this same woman happened to get on stage and speak to us. Although she was presenting some highly pertinent information, I somehow managed to ignore what my spirit was trying to say to me and I tuned her out completely. Little did I know, I would soon find myself sitting in the office of this very same woman I ignored, seeking help that only she could provide.

§

As the days ticked by, I still felt apprehensive about changing my major because I didn't have a single clue as to what I was going to change it to. One evening, I found myself sitting on my bed trying to study for a psychology exam. But, for some reason, I couldn't seem to focus. My mind kept drifting back to my major. This whole "I need to change my major" notion wouldn't give me any peace. Unable to keep studying, I closed my book and pulled out my laptop. Thinking back to the alternative plan in which my tutor had suggested, I searched for jobs that one can get with a bachelor's degree in Biology.

As the results showed up, all I kept seeing were jobs that talked about being in a laboratory, doing some type of research, or looking under a microscope. I'm the type of person that speaks out loud, so I recall myself saying something like, "Oh naww. Justin (my tutor), must be crazy if he thinks I want to be working in somebody's lab fooling with test tubes and petri dishes." Knowing that a life confined to a lab and working with scientific equipment wasn't for me, I shut my laptop and did something I should've done from the beginning. I began to pray. I remember saying,

"Lord, I need your help. I need to change my major, but to what? Lord, I need you to give me some direction." As I finished this very succinct prayer, I vividly recollect seeing two scintillating rays of sunshine pierce through the blinds covering my window. As these rays reached me, it was as if they began to dance across my bed in a spectacular pas de deux. Entranced by this mini light show, I unexpectedly felt a cool breeze gently encircle me; and with this breeze I heard the words "Human Relations". And just as quickly as it all happened, it was over in a blink of an eye. The lights faded, and the breeze ceased to exist.

Call me crazy; call me a liar; call me anything you want, but I know what I heard. This is my story and I'm sticking to it. In Nene Leaks' words, "I said what I said." I immediately knew that God had spoken to me and answered my prayer just that quick. Speaking out loud again, I asked myself, "Human Relations? What in the world is Human Relations? I know I've heard Caroline say it a million times, but what is it exactly?" Still pondering what had just transpired, I went about the rest of my night never stopping to notice that in that moment, my mind was finally at ease. I felt a peace like no other and it suffused through my spirit.

§

The following day, I found myself in Mrs. Carter's office. I couldn't let myself sit there and not ask her for counsel in relation to my major. I came right out and told her, "I need to change my major, but I don't know what to change it to." Her response was, "Well, have you considered Human Relations?" Y'all, my mouth dropped to the floor. I literally had to turn my head to check and see if I was being punk'd! Naturally, I asked, "How did you know I was considering Human Relations? Mind you, I hadn't spoken with anyone about what I experienced the day before. She simply replied, "I didn't, but I just felt led to tell you that." Straightaway, I knew that her response was the divine confirmation I had been looking for. The insidious cloud of confusion and despair, which had been hovering over me for so long, was finally gone. It was in that moment I was truly liberated.

Even after I realized I needed to change my major to Human Relations, I still had one more fish to fry -- my math class. I imagined myself putting this class in the deep fryer like you would some fish, turning the heat to the max, stepping back to avoid the onslaught of grease missiles firing at me, and watching it burn to a bitter crisp. Due to me switching majors, Pre-calculus Trigonometry was no longer a requirement for me. I had to petition the Dean of University College in order to drop the class and receive a "W" (withdrawal) on my transcript. That was much better than the dreadful "F" I undoubtedly would have had I stayed in that class. As soon as I saw that math class disappear from my schedule, I just about passed out in relief. Ebullient. Ecstatic. Elated. Exultant. These are a few words that can accurately describe how I felt knowing that my math taking days were over. It was as if a ginormous weight had been lifted off my bony shoulders by the talons of my favorite animal -- the majestic bald eagle. With the weight gone, I could literally feel strength returning to my body. In a sense, this newfound energy brought me back to life.

CHAPTER 5

Puzzle Piece: Find Your Passion Pt. 5

After Mrs. Carter helped me find a major suited for me, I began to recognize my passion -- passions, rather -- with newfound clarity. Once I was able to remove the money from the equation, and I stopped focusing on earning the coveted six-figure salary, it was then that I came to truly ascertain that my passions had no price tag. I realized that my passions could not simply be defined by dollar signs and monetary value. I understood that my passions were priceless and worth far more than the most precious jewels on earth. In saying that, I want you to know that your own passions are equally as precious and priceless. As hard as it may be in this tremendously capitalistic and money hungry world, you must let the money go. I'm not talking about drop it to the side so that you can pick it back up later. I mean like really let it go. Let it go like Elsa did in "Frozen" -- lol. Just so we're clear, and so that you don't go telling your parents or guardians I said money isn't important, that's not what I'm saying. I know that money is an important factor in life because I'm trying to get these coins too -- lol. What I am saying, however, is not to let money be the sole driving force behind what you want to study, major in, and ultimately make a career out of. Don't allow your success to be defined by how much money you're making. When money is your main tether to reality and functionality, it displaces passion and becomes all consuming. If you find yourself being consumed, allow your passion or passions to become a light in the dark that leads you out of the abyss and back onto your path. Although I may implore you to discover your passion with urgency, from my stories, you know all too well that said discovery can take some time. So, do just that. Take your time, but don't take so long that time passes you by.

During your quest to discover this passion, remember that it's a process. It took me almost a whole semester to figure out that I didn't need to be psychiatrist to operate in my passion. Instead, after I graduate with my bachelor's degree, I plan to go to graduate school. I will pursue a Master's in Human Relations, obtain my license to be a professional counselor, and eventually open my own private practice. Through this avenue, I can still fulfill my passion of wanting to help young people cope with trauma and work through debilitating issues. In addition to that, it wasn't until around December in 2015 that I realized I had a passion for writing -- hence the book you're reading now. I've always been an avid reader, but never in my wildest dreams did I ever envision actually writing a book. Furthermore, it wasn't until my sophomore year in college that I began to cultivate a new passion—working in higher education with both potential and current college students alike. Slowly but surely, as I matriculated from semester to semester and year to year, I continued completing my college/life puzzle with the right pieces that made me feel whole.

By now, you're probably thinking, "There's no way changing his major had such a profound effect on his life." But, in all honesty, it really did. In fact, after I changed my major, my life began to flood with opportunities. These opportunities are ones that I wouldn't have been exposed to, or even considered, had I not come to recognize my passions in life. For example, I started volunteering and eventually interning at the Boys & Girls Club of Norman. I've been fortunate in building genuine rapport with multiple HR faculty and staff, including the chair of the department. I was even afforded the chance to study abroad—twice. To further illustrate, I would've never considered being a Resident Adviser had I not changed my major. When I first heard of the job, I scoffed at the length of the application and swiftly dismissed it. However, after becoming a Human Relations major, I decided that being an RA would present me with an exquisite opportunity to hone my professional HR skills. Three years later, and I am still in this position. I wouldn't even take silver or gold in exchange for having the opportunity to help incoming freshman navigate through both their collegiate and personal experiences. So, I guess you could say that finding my passion through Human Relations was the catalyst that sparked my immaculate metamorphosis. It's what transformed me from a young man unsure of which path to take into an invigorated man ready to walk in his purpose.

CHAPTER 6

Puzzle Piece: Walk in Your Purpose Pt. 1

KNOCK! KNOCK! Are you still there? I hope the answer is yes. And I mean a big yes. Like, I need your "yes" to be the type of yes you would give if someone asked you if you'd like a million dollars. Don't give me that dry as dust "yes" that you give your parents or guardians when they ask you if you're awake for school at 6:30 in the morning. I need you to bear with me for just a moment longer. We need to talk about this thing called **purpose**. What is it? Purpose is something that is vastly ambiguous, yet completely comprehensible. Purpose is something that I've found to be a hidden treasure encompassed by mystique. I know you're probably like, "Eric. Would you quit talking in riddles and just tell me what purpose is?" Am I right? Right or wrong, let me get to the point. In the simplest way I can put it, your purpose is your **why**. I don't mean your **why** as in why you love to do something -- that's passion. I mean your **why** as in the single most important reason you were put on this earth. Whether you're spiritual or not, we all have a purpose. If and when you discover this purpose can be contingent on a few things: the people you surround yourself with, the people you learn from and listen to, and your own willingness to find it. Ultimately, discovering your purpose and truly understanding it is solely up to you. In saying that, coming to understand your purpose, and how to walk in it, is another piece you'll need to complete your puzzle as you matriculate through both college and life itself.

Still a little confused? Let's try it like this. Think of it in terms of a spontaneous road trip to a place you've never been before. Whereas your **passion** is the car you need to arrive at this place, your **purpose** is simultaneously the gas in the tank that fuels your car and it's the destination. Let me break it down even further and use myself as example. Without a shadow of a doubt, I know that I've found my purpose. As I transitioned from a freshman to a senior, it became even clearer. Plain and simple, my purpose is to **inspire**. My purpose is to inspire young adults, particularly students like yourselves. My purpose is to inspire young people to pursue higher education (if this is the best path for them), achieve their dreams by following their passion, and truly understand how essential it is to give back to their communities. Whether it's with time, knowledge, or money, giving back is paramount. If you're reading this and you're not a young adult, I really hope that you can be inspired as well. Although my purpose may be concentrated around the younger generation, my purpose of inspiration has no parameters and you are most definitely included.

Going back to my example of the road trip, my purpose to inspire keeps me going. When the days are rough, and the roads are ragged, my purpose pushes me forward. When the nights get cold, and the journey gets lonely, my purpose provides me with unparalleled warmth and companionship. Though my purpose is fueling me from within, that unknown destination is also still my purpose. What lies in store for me at this destination is still a mystery. You may be wondering, "How is the destination still a mystery Eric if you already know your purpose?" Well, it's still a mystery because I honestly don't know what to expect once I arrive at this destination. To arrive at this destination would mean I've "completed" my purpose. And what this "completion" will look like exactly, I'm not sure. In other words, until I fulfill my purpose, this equivocal destination will remain clandestine. However, I will say this. Whatever happens when I reach my destination, and fulfill my purpose, I will be content. And when you discover your own purpose, I encourage you to accept the fulfillment of your purpose with the alacrity of an angel.

In summation, describing what purpose is, is the easy part. How you unlock its secrets and uncover its meaning is a whole other ball game. Hang in there with me for a little while longer. I'm almost done. If you need to grab you a little something to eat or a little something to drink, go ahead and do so. I want you to be as comfortable as possible going forward. That being said, I hope you brought your uniforms, your tennis shoes, your tennis racquet, some more water and a towel for this "whole other ball game" because it's time to play ball!

CHAPTER 7

Puzzle Piece: Walk in Your Purpose Pt. 2

Now that you (hopefully) understand what purpose is, we need to discuss how we find it. Although finding your own unique purpose will be up to you, I hope to help you by sharing how I found my own.

If you recall, I told you that I'm passionate about working with students -- especially in the realm of higher education. I also told you that I'm passionate about writing. Well, as I cultivated my passion for working with these students, my purpose became more evident. As a freshman, I volunteered to help with a conference called the George McLaurin and Sylvia A. Lewis Leadership Conference. At first, I was hesitant about helping because I didn't know too much about the conference or what I should expect. I initially had made up my mind not to volunteer. What many of you don't know is that once I have made my mind up not to do something, it's pretty much set in stone. It's another one of those, "I said what I said" type of things. That said, my friends know this about me and yet they still tried to convince me to get involved. One of my best friends, Michala Davis, just kept on insisting that I do it. Y'all, she was like this little bothersome bug that wouldn't quit flying around my face. When I tell you I was ready to get the fly swatter and pop her out of the sky, I was ready to POP her – lol.

Have y'all ever told somebody something and they don't agree with it, so they go and bring somebody else to you to try and prove why they're right? Well, that's exactly what she did. We were on the phone talking about the conference when Michala had the nerve to go and get this guy named J.D. and put him on the phone. Mind you, I didn't know this man whatsoever. Despite the unexpected conversation, we talked for almost 30 minutes. I learned that he, like myself (at that time), was once selected to receive the President's Outstanding Freshman Award. To make a long story short, he basically told me that not many people of color receive such a prestigious honor, and that the students who would be attending that conference needed to meet a student like me.

By the end of our conversation, the motto I walked away with is one that is quite familiar to students at The University of Oklahoma. If I mention Soonerthon, I'm pretty sure you can guess what it is. For those of you who are reading this, and are unfamiliar with Soonerthon, the motto they use is FTK, "For the Kids." After our conversation, it just dawned on me. Volunteering at this conference wasn't about me, it was about the kids. It was about the students whose lives I could impact. Needless to say, I changed my mind and decided to volunteer at the conference. I have never regretted that decision. In addition to this conference, Mrs. Carter, my amazing adviser, encouraged me to volunteer at two other conferences hosted by the Oklahoma Police Department's F.A.C.T. (Family Awareness Community Teamwork) Program: "We Rise" (for young ladies) and "Man Up" (for young men). For a lack of better words, my overall sense of fulfillment was absolutely astonishing.

After volunteering at each of these conferences, I felt extraordinarily complete. Year after year, I was able to see the real difference I was making the lives of these students. It wasn't until after my second year of volunteering, that the light bulb came on in my head. I had students call me or ask to meet up. Sometimes, they told me that I was the reason they decided to choose OU. Other times, they told me that I inspired them to become a leader on campus. As much as I hate verbal words of affirmation, something inside of me clicked. It was during these moments that I realized that my **purpose** was to inspire. Just so you know, to this day, I still volunteer at each of these conferences in addition to working summer camps like OU Upward Bound and Find Your Future Camp. My sense of fulfillment and wholeness continues to overflow like the torrential current of a river cascading rapidly, yet beautifully, over a steep precipice.

To further illustrate how I found my purpose, I want to reiterate how important becoming a Resident Advisor was. This role was so pivotal, that without it, I couldn't have come up with this book's title. Better yet, I wouldn't even be writing this book. All in all, being an RA for the 2nd floor in DLB (David L. Boren Hall) and Walker 7 West completely transformed my life. The residents of both floors gave me something to live for. They accentuated the clarity of my purpose. In this position, I realized that so many students, whether they were rich or poor, black, white, blue, green, or purple, needed guidance. They wanted help deciding what major they should choose and if that major was the right fit. Yes, they wanted that major to help them make some money; however, they also really wanted to find a major that would also enable them to authentically be happy. Because of them, I started writing this book as opposed to the fiction novel I was already working on. With all of this in mind, by combining my passion for writing and my passion for students, I began to walk in my purpose -- meaning, I was actively working in it. Thus, the publishing of this very book was a direct result of the unbelievable synergy of my **passion** and **purpose**.

CONCLUSION

It's been said time and time again: you need to know what you want to do before you get to college. They say that the main reason you need to go to college is so that you can get a degree that will allow you to make a lot of money. I must admit, I too, believed these statements to be true once upon a time -- but no longer.

If you read through this entire book, and you've made it this far, neither should you. Whether you go to college or not, I want you to turn the last page of this book knowing that you have a purpose in life. I want you to close this book understanding that when you find your passion and follow it, you will be okay. I did **not** say you will be rich, so do **not** go around lying on me and telling folks I said that following your passion will make you rich. Now, that's not to say it can't happen. I'm just saying not to blame me if it doesn't happen. What I **did** say, however, is that you will be okay. So far, following my passion hasn't made me rich, but it has opened doors of opportunity that I never imagined possible.

I fully believe that your passion will make room for you to be financially, academically, and emotionally fulfilled. By "make room" I mean that your passion will aid you in the areas listed above. Taking it a step further, once you find your purpose, it will sustain you. When encountering low times in your life that make you want to throw in the towel, your purpose will step in and help you pick yourself back up again. When you feel as if you are at the top of your game and can't go any higher, your purpose will propel you to even greater heights. In other words, your purpose is strength and hope incarnate. You can always trust in your purpose. It's not that you can't trust your passion, you just have to be aware of the fact that it can change depending on the scenario. This is particularly likely for those of us who have multiple passions. Honestly, it really comes down to you knowing who you are.

If you ever find yourself confusing the two, remember this: **passion can ebb and flow. It can change like water. But purpose? Purpose is finite, concrete, and individually unique. It can't be changed or replicated.**

All things considered, I promise this is actually the end of my book. I'm not going to spring another story or two on you -- lol. I would also like to personally thank you for taking the time to read it. Given all that you have read, I want you know that no matter what anyone says, you are **ENOUGH**. In all that you do, **BELIEVE** in yourself. I believe in you and I'm rooting for you. It's my hope, prayer, and wish for you to understand that all of the **right** pieces needed to complete your puzzle of college/life are already within **you**. And among these pieces, the two most important are passion and purpose. As you proceed with your journey, if things stop working out or something starts to feel off, consider this: although you have the right pieces, you might just be trying to place them into the wrong puzzle.

This particular journey may have come to an end, but we will simply just start a new one...

Stay tuned for the next installment in this series: Right Pieces, Wrong Puzzle: The Power of Community and Mentorship

ABOUT THE AUTHOR

Eric Anthony Rollerson was born on October 9, 1996 in Oklahoma City, Oklahoma. Though he was primarily raised by his paternal grandparents, his parents and siblings have always been a major a part of his life. Throughout his life, Eric's family, friends, and teachers have always believed he was going to be incredibly successful in every aspect of his life.

Eric will be obtaining his Bachelor's degree in Human Relations, with a minor in Nonprofit Organizational Studies from The University of Oklahoma, in May 2019. Following his graduation, Eric will pursue his Master's in Human Relations, with an emphasis in counseling to earn his license to become a professional counselor (LPC). Furthermore, Eric plans to start both his own business and a nonprofit organization.

Eric is the reigning Mister Black OU 2018-2019. His platform is: **Be A Light, Make A Change**. Through his platform, Eric utilizes the light God has given him to inspire youth by accentuating his philosophy of **Ex3: Exposure, Empowerment, Empathy**. His goal is to inspire these youth to become better versions of themselves, stand up for what they believe in, and fight for their futures. It is his hope that these same youth will one day pour jewels of experience and wisdom back into future young minds.

As an extension of his platform, Eric organized OU's inaugural Royal Ball. The Royal Ball is a philanthropic event in which the proceeds were donated to the Boys & Girls Club of Norman, a nonprofit he deeply cherishes. Even more so, Eric created a program called "The Shadow Project." This program gives first-generation and/or economically disadvantaged students the free opportunity to experience life as a college student. The students get to shadow OU college students in the classroom while also receiving information from various campus resources. Though the process of creating and executing these two phenomenal accomplishments was far from easy, the pieces eventually found themselves being seamlessly put together into the perfect puzzle. Even still, there is so much more in store for Eric as he continues his journey in life.

Made in the USA
Middletown, DE
07 January 2021